FANTASY, DREAMS
BATTLES & MAGIC

an illustrated poetry collection

Book copyright 2015 by Jon H. Gutmacher

Published by:
Jon H. Gutmacher, P.A.
1861 South Patrick Drive
Indian Harbour Beach, Florida 32937
Phone: 407-279-1029
email: gutlaw@gmail.com

Copyrights & Permissions

Cover illustration: Celtic Princess by Gaston Bussiere (1911)

Table of Contents

Table of Illustrations

Table of Illustrations – continued

Introduction

I started writing poetry back in junior high school when introduced to it in an English class. I remember reading "The Charge of the Light Brigade" by Lord Tennyson, and being totally blown away by it. Who knew poetry could be about battles? Prior to that I thought it was just about flowers, romance, and everything else a fourteen year old could care less about. But, I found out it could be much, much more. And, as I matured – so did my expanse of interests. During that time I dabbled in occasionally writing poetry, although my main love was music. In fact, while living in the Miami area prior to graduating college – I actually wrote a weekly poetry column for a local newspaper named The Ojus Sun until the paper went out of business. (Hopefully, not because of my poetry). After that, I stopped writing, and concentrated on getting thru school.

Of course, fantasy has always been my favorite form of reading. The first book I ever read was "The Boys King Arthur", and the stories about King Arthur and his knights flooded my imagination, and began a lifetime love of fantasy, and Sword and Sorcery stories. In fact, until I entered law school, I was a voracious reader of every fantasy and science fiction book I could get my hands on. But, law school stopped all of that. The study of law is a full time experience, and left little time for anything else. That is – until 2010.

In 2010 I experienced a rotator cuff tear. It continued to get worse, until I needed surgery – and the surgery resulted in even more of an injury. The pain was unbearable, and to get through the day I was put on heavy narcotic medication. Even that wasn't much of a help. It took six months before I could handle the pain without meds, and it left my right shoulder pretty useless. It changed my life, and changed my outlook on life. I decided there were more important things in life besides law, and began writing poetry again – probably as a method of self healing.

What I wrote were mostly fantasy poems – sword and sorcery. Brave men who stood against all odds. Beautiful women trapped by magic and evil. Situations in allegory – where I would write a fantasy poem based on a modern event, but place the characters in a fantasy world where good battled evil. Where magic, dragons, and swords ruled. It filled a huge gap in my life, and as I started to write again – I realized that besides the satisfaction it gave me – I was pretty good at it.

That led to the next step – the desire – or more correctly – the need to have someone else see what I was writing. Without an audience – there was no point to what I was doing. I decided to create a website, and began to design it. However, the most important part of the website, aside from the poetry, was that every poem would have a background image that would set the mood of the poem. To do that took months of searching the web, trying to find suitable images. And, of course – having a great web designer (David Cate from Orlando Web Development) to partner in the design of the site, and put my ideas into reality was critical.

The result was that within the first ten months of its creation, the site (fantasypoetrybyjongutmacher.com) was ranked as one of the top two "fantasy poetry" websites in the nation by Google, and it has stayed that way since 2011, being ranked either #1 or #2 on a consistent basis in that genre.

So, what do you do after creating a successful website with your poems? You write a book of them, or at least, I did. While I have no illusions about the book being a best seller – hopefully, it will allow my poetry to spread beyond just the web. It's something I love. And hopefully, you'll love them, as well.

FANTASY, DREAMS, BATTLES & MAGIC

an illustrated poetry collection

From me to you, and so you see
The sky, the moon
The rising sea
And dream the dream
If dreams can be
Welcome to my fantasy
world

Illustration: The Coming of Lancaster by the
American painter and illustrator, Howard Pyle.
(1908). The poem, "The Good King", is an allegory
honor, courage and loyalty, and the plight of those
returning troops who fall on hard times, some
becoming homeless, and what is truly owed to
them for their sacrifice. (2011).

The Good King and Faithful Knight

On fateful day the king rode out
to see the land
and those about
to gauge the temperament
of what He held
to survey the realm
to serve it well

And at this time
not far away
a man grew weak
no place to stay

He lived on roots
and what he could steal
for this (was) his only way
to have a meal

Once a warrior
brave and true
T'were many an enemy
that he slew
and once he saved
his enbattled King
and fought all who would
invade the Land

But age and times
can be quite hard
and men forget the past . . .
and youth
it does not last

No place to live
no life to feel
except old wounds
that would not heal

The cold, dark nights
so empty, bleak
life passed him by
his eyes grew weak

But when he heard
the king approached
he hobbled to
the hedge, and broached
and proudly stood to glimpse his Liege
then bowed his head
to knee

The King passed by
and then stopped dead
for something swooned
inside his head
and then reared back
His eyes looked deep
He saw the man
and had to speak

"I know you, friend
I know you well
You fought beside me
And fought like hell
You saved my life
more times than once
is this how I reward?

And then He alighted
from his stead
and joined the man
on bended knee
and raised him up
eye to eye
and stopped a tear
for Kings
don't cry

"To you I give
a home and land
and funds enough
for you to stand
for all your days a man of wealth
whose Liege remembers
well"

And then the warrior
who once was bold
but now just tatters
and so so old
raised fist to heart in deep salute
and looked at King
so resolute

"You do me honor
you've paid the debt
and for all of time with deep respect
for when I saved you
that battled day
I knew this then
and still I say

"There never was
a better king than you
I would do it all again"

And the warrior lived
the life he should
and on his grave
this inscription stood:

"He served thru life
A grateful king
who never
will forget"

Illustration: Queen Yseult by the French Symbolist painter, Gaston Bussiere. (1911). My comments on the inspiration for the poem come at its conclusion.

Snow White — the poem.

The Queen so fair
the mirror bright
it says her name
but thinks Snow White

For evil lies
in heart so black
and nothing will it stay

Her beauty reigns
in castle tall
but hidden dark
behind its walls

Lie spells and magic
as dark as night
with gloom and death
no, nothing's –
right

For she the Queen
of darkness all
rules by death
and magic pall

She questions the mirror
again this day
"Who is the fairest
"Who is, I say?"

"My queen, you are the fairest now
"no one compares
"nor, you allow
"but beauty runs beyond skin deep
"and in these things your blackness keep
"but yes, behold, you are most fair
"your beauty reigns supreme"

The Queen looked puzzled at the vow
but thought not much
not then . . . but now
for all she saw was that to see
her beauty great
oh, that it be

And went to hall
where knights bowed down
her subjects groveled all around
and gawked and looked
her beauty fair
for she was much to see

Her body tight
her skin so pure
her eyes so blue like deep azure
and hair so black like heart not seen
a face so fair
quite like a dream

But deep within that heart of stone
lived a hell that she called home
for jealous to an inch of life
let none oppose
lest die in strife

With poisoned eyes and poisoned spells
and poisoned potions
from poisoned wells
her evil vision could see thru stone
this Queen who rules this Land

And so the days turned into night
and time passed on with each dawn's light
and sent her armies far and wide
until she ruled all country sides

And all did homage to this Queen
who broke her enemies
through force and scheme

For none could stand against her now
Her powers stood all tests

"Now mirror, mirror on the wall
"Who is the fairest of us all?
"Who rules the land
"Who rules from hell
"Who casts bold spells
"That none can quell?"

"T'is you, my queen, who is most fair
"With azure eyes and flowing hair
"But Snow White lives and now grows tall
"her beauty deep
"will be your fall"

For when she turns but twenty one
"Your life will end
"Your reign undone
"And Prince from far will take your Land
"their love will make her queen!"

The Queen turned black
Her rage drew flames
She screamed with hate at Snow White's name
and vowed to cut pure heart from breast
"Until that's done
"I shall not rest!"

And ran to Hall
her knights they bowed
and brought the huntsman
from where t'was found
and ordered him that very day

to seek Snow White who he would slay
to cut her heart from beating breast
and place it then
in small jeweled chest

"Then bring her heart that I can see
"that Snow White's death
"is sure!!"

The huntsman thought to ask but why
But knew to ask then he would die
So simply bowed with fist to chest
to do her bidding on this black quest
and left the Hall
and set on out
to obey his evil Queen

He'd heard Snow White
her beauty, true
did live in woods
where not . . . he knew
but searched the lands until one day
he heard her name
"Snow White"
they say

Is purer than an evening star
her smile warms all from near and far
and hair so black
and lips so red
with perfect body
is what they said

And there she was in clearing light
her smile shown
her eyes were bright
and pure as pure a gentle stream
no hint of bad
no stroke of mean

She looked at him as he approached
his blade came out
he grabbed her throat
but then her goodness overcame
he dropped the knife
his hands went lame

"Oh, Princess . . . I cannot!
"For you are so fair
"I cannot harm one precious hair
"You are so pure
"you are so good
"I see why she wants you dead."

And then the huntsman
told her all
And Snow White turned
an ashen pall
"Now hide – or die
as quick can be
"I'll slay a pig for Queen
to see
"For if she ever
finds the truth
"we'll both pay with our lives!"

And deep the forest did she go
where fainted dead
in morning snow
and seven dwarfs did find her there
and took her to their home

And there she lived
for most three years
their steadfast love
quelled all her fears
until one day the Queen arrived
with apple in her hand

And dwarfs were gone
she could not see
the evil witch that Queen could be
and took a bite
then felt the death
but cried one time to dwarfs in west

They heard her cry thru forest and trees
and grabbed their weapons
and ran with speed
and saw the Queen
and cut her down
and cried aloud at what they found

Snow White lay dead upon the snow
yet still in death she held a glow
so pure her beauty
so pure her heart
they could not accept
they could not part

So built a box of glass so fair
and placed her in with loving care
and in a clearing
for all to see
her beauty never waned

And years they passed
until one day
she'd be twenty one
or so . . . all say
and on that day a Prince so bold
who heard the tale
that many told
and rode his horse
into the clear
and lifted glass
then pressed her near

For he was great and magic, too
and in his heart he always knew
that he would find her
on that day and kissed the lips
swept death away

And watched her color begin to grow
her eyes they opened
at first – so slow
For love had triumphed where death had not
as all around dwarfs cheered!

He took her to his land as queen
then joined their lands and those between
and all rejoiced
and all was well
for the Land was now
at peace

epilog:

"Oh, mirror, mirror
"On the wall
"Who is the fairest
"Of them all?

Snow White – The Poem: Snow White started as an experiment whether I could write a full length poem from an existing story. It took almost a week to finish, and has become the top ranked poem on my website. It's original inspiration came while watching the coming attractions for the 2012 film "Snow White and the Huntsman", although the poem had nothing to do with the film.   (2012)

Illustration: Prague, copyright Shukaylova Zinaida, at Shutterstock, by license. The poem, "Tasmerelda", was my first modern fantasy poem, the one that started all the rest. A story of good vs. evil where an evil magician manipulates all. The ending line, deliberately written in both past and future tense, asks if the story is just legend, or true? And if true, will Tasmerlda ever be rescued? (2010)

Tasmerelda – A Fairytale?

En Tigeray, es Tasmerelda
yearning err the Hooded Elder
and the Knight who rides in white
sighs Tasmerelda through the night

As tapestries sway back and forth
the midnight breeze comes blowing forth
and White Knight stands near hooded horror
Calling eerie through her parlor

To Tasmerelda, where she be
She sighs and moans to be set free
and White Knight thrusts with sharpened blade
the eerie sounds at last are stayed

Tis Tasmerelda at last set free?

But no, he falters
the blade is stopped
and hooded in his eerie frock
The magic plays
The music strays
and White Knight falls to blood fate grave

And all is silent
Yes, all is lost
and moaning from her tower loft
cries Tasmerelda for one last time
Now mist and vines begin to climb

Eer castle, tower, all in all
the spell is woven, the gatemen fall

And all asleep forever more
in tangled garments, and vine tossed lore

Was Tasmerelda ever be?

Illustration: Painting by the French Symbolist painter, Gaston Bussiere. The poem is the epilogue to Tasmerelda, and tells the story of what became of her. But, as in Tasmerelda — not all things end as they should. For while all rejoice in her rescue by a brave knight – Evil still watches. (2011)

The Legend of Evermore

She sleeps in snow white death . . .
a hundred years of time pass into nothing
for who remembers her?
except for those who perished with her?

A legend?
a myth?
a figment of imagination or time?

No air
no breath
no passing light
and does she even dream . . .
and if so of what?

"Of what? ", you ask
of things you've never seen
or dreamed, or felt

For once there was, or so they say
and now what is has gone its way
And even magic cannot it stay
for the legend called "Evermore"

And so time passes
each day alighting into tomorrow
and the cooling breeze flows freely
across the moonlite clouds

But no one
not a soul
still remembers the beauty that She was
the perfection that She held
the touch of her hand
the depth of her laugh
the warmth of her smile
the truth in her heart

For ancient vines surround her now
the castle down
the gatemen all
and everything she loved and more
they do not now exist

Who placed this curse on perfect brow?
is it to last?
or end it now?
or is it spent
or will it be
is there an answer for us to see?

That is the question I know you ask
so I put to you
this final task:

To determine the answer
the truth you seek
the shadowed past
that truth might speak

For what was Once
and now is now
and time stands still
as He allows
And so we fall into the chasm
the deep abyss
to add unto that ancient list

Of unknown curses, and unknown tales
of unknown spells, unanswered wails
of maidens
dragons
mage and death
the clang of armor
unending quest

For hundred years has passed this day
the mist recedes, vines pull away
and in the distance none can believe
the tower stands
the gatemen breathe

And now the Knight 'stride golden steed
even as the rest recedes
and takes her in his arms so slow
her breath and color begin to glow
and magic kiss that only He
could come to pass bestow on She
and so for all and Evermore
the story ends no longer lore

The ending that all hoped to see
Has finally come
and set her free

And so it ends yet begins anew
for all and Evermore

(epilogue:)

But somewhere . . .
someplace dark and dread
the sorcerer rears his sleeping head
and sees thru time what all has passed
and now decides
if all things last

For Evermore will never be
no life is perfect
or so you'll see

Yet time will pass
while life goes on
and on
for Evermore

Illustration: Lancelot and Guinevere by the great American illustrator, N.C. Wyeth. (1908). My inspiration came while watching news stories of the rescue of two kidnapping victims, Jaycee Durgard and Elizabeth Smart. The story is an allegory about the terror and tragedy caused by kidnapping. (2011)

Arriella – and the Evil Magician

Arriella! . . . Arriella!
Oh, where have you gone?
you were here just today
by tall castle . . . 'yon
with gold flowing hair
with white flowing dress
with fairies to guide you
with talisman at your breast

Who took you?
Who managed to get thru the spells?
to weave through your guards
all wishing you well

The king is asunder
the queen is in tears
the Mage casting spells
through all of his fears

But none have yet seen you
the castle grows dim
your joy now has left us
our heads all do swim

For all of us failed you
your joy has moved out
our knights all on quest
"No rest!" do we shout!

We'll find you!
We swear it!
Not one of us rest!
Our meals now are meager
for all on your quest

To travel the earth
to scour the halls
to seek out that Evil that caused this great pall

And one day we'll find you
and all will rejoice
the land will reap flowers
our halls fill with noise

For our beautiful princess was taken away
by an Evil Magician
or, that's what they say

And now as I ride
my sword at my hilt
I pass through a wood
this chill Now I've felt

That never . . .
That never . . .
I've yet felt before . . .

My hairs stand on end
my chest tightens, too
my hand grasps my sword
my shield falls askew

For there in a clearing chained to a tree
is Arriella, my princess
I fall to one knee

But, I know to be silent
I know it's a trap
and if I do fail
She'll never be back

And so, with all stealth
as quiet as can be
I take out the cloak the Mage gave to me

And place it on, over
as I vanish from view
the magic has power
my sword shall it slew

And then I do chant what Mage told to me
it works only once to set Arriella free

And so, in an instant I see what's foretold
the Evil One there
his black robes so bold

And 'fore he could turn my sword did it swing
his head flew off gruesome
I grabbed off his ring

His powers were ended
His life was undone
And Arriella swooned as I came on the run

And when she awoke I bowed once, so low
she cried for an instant
and then we did go

And placed her on horse
and took her back home
where trumpets rejoiced
no longer alone

And King weak with joy
and Queen full of tears
the halls filled with light
the fairies appeared

And long did we revel
And long did it last
for our Princess was back
yes . . . finally
at last

Illustration: "Dolores", a photograph by the great
Vogue fashion photographer, Adolf De Meyer (1919).
"The Good Witch" is an allegory of how unshakable
religious beliefs and intolerance can cause great harm,
and misunderstanding. (2011)

The Good Witch and Errant King

There was a king in far off land
a godly man as religions stand
who said his prayers
never took things light
but thought, too much
that he was right

A bishop did come fore him once
and told of witches
an evil hunch
that they were damned and caused all harm
and thus incited a great alarm

The king prayed long
for an answer true
and then took knights and witches slew
and those who hid
and those who fled
were the only witches who were not dead

"And now I've rid them from the land
The crops will grow
all witch be damned!"

The bishop smiled
the people prayed
at last from nothing
they were saved

And the witches who
once roamed the land
doing good by spell and hand
were few and far
now secret, too
so very few
the people
knew

Then Evil came with good witch gone
and took the land
and smote it on
and drought and cold
and disease ran thru
the kingdom suffered
as no one knew

And bishop came to castle gate
and then at throne
could hardly wait
to cast more blame
who did not pray
it was – Them
who caused
this blackened
day

And so King passed then
several laws
And threw in chains
some hundred more
and tortured those who would not pray
so each could see
their Evil way

And now the people were truly sad
too many laws that made them mad
but nothing did protect the land
the pestilence still
was out of hand

"Oh, Bishop – what is left to do?
I have listened twice to only you
My kingdom dies
the livestock low
the people sick
the crops
won't grow

The Bishop shook his head but twice
he didn't know
had no advice
could only pray
could only bow
would nothing stop the pestilence now?

And then the Queen came down with pain
a sickly look like ashen rain
the joy she was
it was no more
the church bells rang
her death at store

The King so low
despondent now
for all got worse
no fields to plow
and then a dream came on one night
it lit the room
it set him right

"Tomorrow we go
into the wood!
A dream has told
of witches good
that they are not the evil
that we thought
but heal the land
What have I wrought?"

And on that morn
the King, one knight
they braved thick forest
to get it right
and there so deep
and there so dark
a simple cottage
the King did hark

"I mean no harm
No harm will come
A dream did show . . .
Please, do not run!
And all this time . . .
I've been so wrong
you've hidden here
too long, too long"

And then the witch
came into view
so fair and kind
he surely knew
what Bishop told
was ah, so wrong
his laws were bad
his people wronged

"I am no witch as witch you know
I heal the sick in rain and snow
you killed my kind
as witches go . . .
but I will heal your queen!"

And with a wave of magic hand
a change did come across the land
and all the sick
and all the blight
did vanish in a stroke of light

The King bowed down
a humbled man
and said the words
as best he can:
"I've done you wrong
"I've killed your kind
"While all through time
"You were so kind

"I revoke the laws
"I restore your place
"I open my kingdom
"I accept disgrace
"And never will this happen twice
"Forgive me, please
"Give your advice"

And then she smiled
and flowers grew
twelve fairies appeared
and then He knew
that the Land needed magic for it to stay
for it was magic that kept
the evil away

And from that time no witch was burned
for hence there was a lesson learned
that those with Power
are mainly good
they're sheltered deep
in thickest wood

They protect the land
Protect the peace
Keep pestilence out
beyond Evil's reach
And those who dwell
are only good
if They, you need
go deep
in wood

For if your heart
is straight and true
then only good
will
witches do

Illustration: "Futuristic Alien Planet" copyright by diversepixel, licensed from Fotolia. My commentary appears at the end of the poem.

The Seven Moons of Dargoor

The Time Lord stood at the threshold of the chasm
On His right stood the Minions of Darkness
Armed with hate
and fear
and loathing
ready for battle

For this was no ordinary day
It was the start or the end
of the world

And the Time Lord was there
watching, deciding

For too,
The Forces of Good stood at the ready
their banners blew strong in the wind
snapping in defiance to the cruelty of battle
that would surely decide
who lived
who died
and what would come to pass

And in that moment
that split second before their forces joined
in rage and death
the Time Lord made a decision:

No battle would be had
No world would be destroyed
No death would occur
Not even the slightest shed of blood would occur

For He had the Power
and though rarely used
sometimes what was right and good
was more important than what was written

And so – looking into their hearts
He chose a man from the Forces of Evil
and a woman from the Forces of Good

Both warriors
Both heros
Both renowned amongst their peers
And joined them together to rule both

And though the hate of the races was real
So the Time Lord gave them love
a thing that was more real
a thing so lasting that nothing
could stand before it

And chose five hundred of the best warriors
from either side
And made them swear allegiance
to their new King and Queen

And the Time Lord then appeared before Them all
and told them of His decision

And there was silence for a long time
and then suddenly
with the clamor of their swords ringing on their shields
Their voices rose as one
for a new future
where love would rule
rather than hate and fear

And the gloom of the mist that had hung
long and low over the battlefield
disappeared
and the Seven Moons of Dargoor
shown together
in perfect alignment
. . . as They do now
every one hundred years

And on that date
A New World began
That lasts even today
and is the History of Our Peoples

So the story of Dargoor
and how the Time Lord
saved us from ourselves
so long, long ago

The Seven Moons of Dargoor is one of my few free verse poems. It started out purely as a love poem, and took on a life of its own, quite unexpected, for the characters would not do what I wanted them to do – and though I had planned a battle – the character of the Time Lord would not allow it. The Time Lord is a God, or a supernatural guardian of a world in chaos. While he watches, the planet prepares for global war of the two dominant races. A war that will spell the annihilation of one, or both. The Time Lord, who sees all, decides that despite Free Will — he will not allow these beings to destroy themselves — and so introduces love to both the races — something stronger and more lasting than their mutual hate — and by doing so, not only saves the planet — but changes its course, forever. The story ends when you realize that it is being told to you, as a descendant of one of the original Peoples, on the hundredth year anniversary of the Star Lord's intervention — and the additional gift given by Him as an eternal reminder — the perfect alignment of all of Dargoors seven moons — which happens, on this fateful anniversary, only once – every hundred years.   (2011)

Illustration: From the book "The White Company",
painted by N.C. Wyeth. (1922). The poem tells the
story of a great battle when Viking raiders invade.
Only luck finds them in time, and the King rushes to
set a trap resulting in a great battle and victory. The
tactics involved are taken from three separate major
battles of the ancient world. It is an allegory of
courage, and a representation that only those brave
enough to fight for what they believe, survive the
onslaught. (2011)

The Battle of the Coastal Raiders

Thru the clearing he did go
bow at ready
sword in tow

There a ship upon the rise
full of warriors
huge surprise

"Warn the others while I stay!
use all speed to get away
Bring the army!
Bring the knights!
Make them march throughout the night!

"Tell the king
the enemy's here
armed with swords
both shield, and spear

"A hundred in each ship I see
four ships have landed
I still count three!"

The squire ran
as hard, he could
thru the trees and thru the wood

Thru the fields
to castle gate
there collapsed
but not too late

Gasping
Gasping
weak with pain
breathing heavy
almost lame

"Raiders, come!
They've come by boat
Seven hundred to kill and smote
My Knight is waiting
He spied them all
Hurry, Sire
Lest all we fall"

"To Arms! To Arms!
bring kingdom out!
Gather the archers
the King did shout!
Put on your swords
Grab lance and shield
Take none alive
and do not yield!

"For this is not a game we play
it is survival, or we die, this day
I know these scum who invade our land
they kill all men
and let nothing stand

"They rape the women
keep those most fair
the rest are killed without a care
all homes are burned
the castles torn
they steal the livestock
they burn the corn

"The children are
all kept as slaves
to tend their fields
to serve their games
to sacrifice
to beat with pain
we stop them here
Our Gods, ordain!"

"My King
the army is assembled now
one thousand strong
as you allow
Three hundred bows
two hundred horse
the rest with sword
it's quite a force

"What order, Lord?
What now we do?
How will the battle
be planned by you?"

"We cannot meet them on the beach
their ships have landed
their lines be neat
an ambush must we somehow make
take archers hence
and put up stakes

"For as they pass
on yonder road
they'll come thru clearing
where we – untold
will have our archers
hidden at either side
we'll take them fast
'fore they can hide
and once our arrows take their toll
with sword and horse
we'll run them cold"

And so the plan was made to be
and huntsmen left so silently
to watch the foe
to kill their scouts
to report to King
and set the rout

And everything did go as planned
the Raiders came thru road and land
and in the clearing they were met
with arrows
they would not forget

And men were pierced
and horses too
their shields were down
before they knew
that ambushed well
oh that, they be
they died by hundreds
for all to see

And then the army
with swords draw out
came thru the wood
with one great shout
and charged the confusion
like a wall of steel
their swords like talons
with death did deal

The invaders crumbled
and began to flee
and then the knights charged forcefully
at full gallop horse
they ran them down
the blood flowed free
as hoofs did pound

Not one, was spared that bloody day
their ships were burned
none got away
and when the King
came on the field
the carnage there
so bloody real

"So, this – the lesson that we teach
Our kingdom safe
beyond harm's reach
For today you've saved your land
and King
Your families live
Now minstrels sing

"For feast we will
this bloody night
for we survived
the awful fight

"Our children live
our crops grow tall
our women laugh
our enemies fall

"And every year this Raider Day
We'll remember well
and each will say:
"That vigilance will protect us all
"Lest our land
"and kingdom fall"

"For we stood and fought
where others flee
and because of that
we still are free

"And Kingdom
ah, this blessed land
these castle walls
they hold!"

Illustration: Section from painting "The Battle of Grunwald" by the Polish painter, Jan Matzjeko. (1874). The poem tells of a knight who spares the life of a dwarf, and is later rewarded when the dwarf saves the knight, his queen, and entourage. An allegory that all persons and creatures should be treated with respect. (2011)

Dwarf King

Once, long ago a valiant knight
was in the forest at dawn's first light
and stealthful as a knight could be
he spied a dwarf behind a tree

Oh, what a treasure, what a find
to capture one of this rare kind
the Lords and Ladies would gather round
and slap his back at what he found

He drew his bow with arrow true
but dwarf did see before he slew
Did shout to knight behind a tree
"Oh, spare me, Sir. Let me go free!"

The knight relaxed
the bow went down
and gazing with a piercing frown
did ask the dwarf "why", he should?
"Now, tell me, Dwarf!
"And make it good"

"I am a King amongst my kind
"I'll owe you, Sir, and you will find
"that always will you have my ear
"and in these woods you'll never fear."

The knight, he nodded
held high his hand
then walked away back to his land
and went in thru the castle gates
and kept the story for his own sake

Until one day traveling through the wood
guarding Queen and ladies just as he should
on lonely road a bit too late
to castle far where others wait

But there were varlets in ambush deep
no care of knights or those they keep
to take the queen and ladies fair
to ransom them without a care

The arrows came, two knights went down
He drew his sword
His heart did pound
He saw them come upon the run
He swung his sword
now two were done

The queen did scream
her ladies, too
they were surrounded there
and then he knew . . .
he would be slain, his duty lost
his companions slaughtered
oh, what a cost!

And then an amazing thing occurred
a shout was heard throughout the wood
and hundreds with both shield and spear
the dwarfs came out without a fear

They slew the varlets
they slew them good
they freed the queen
helped as they could
patched wounded knights with magic paste
saved all of them from horrid fates

And then Dwarf King came thru the crowd
and said in voice that was so proud
"You spared my life
"Now, I've saved your queen
"This . . . is something that you've seen.

"Remember, hence for all your sake
"as you pass by our sacred lake
"The friends you made, whoever be
"Are friends for life
"So, let it be!"

And then as quick as they appeared
they vanished all 'cept King, who neared
and grasped the arm of knight he saved
and pointed round at all that laid

"I told you then you'd not regret
for in these woods
for now, and yet
I honor what I said that day
Now, the debt is yours
How will you pay?

And the knight went down
unto one knee
Held out his sword, and said, to He
"I wronged you, Sir, though I set you free
"I thought you not as good as me
"But, I was wrong, I know that now
"You have my friendship if you, allow

And so, the Dwarf King nodded twice
extended hand
shook like a vice
and the two forever knew
that they were friends for life

And every feast this tale is told
of once a knight
who was so bold
but spared a dwarf
thus saved a queen
in the Kingdom
of Farsporlant

Illustration: Midsummer Eve by the English painter, Edward Robert Hughes. (1908) As for the poem, have you ever wondered if fairies, tree spirits, and all those other things of legend actually ever existed, or were they just a made up story?   The "Doubting Knight" was written for pure fun simply to state the open question of whether these tales are based on fact or merely myth, legend, or pure fantasy. (2011)

The Doubting Knight and Fairies

"Who says that fairies do not exist?"
Said Queen to knight, who laughed
For in the wood most every night
their spirits come and pass!

"Oh, Majesty, my life is yours
but certainly, you must see
that fairies are a joke of time
as legends are prone to be!"

"Then come with me this very night
into the wood we'll go
and you will see your errant ways
as fairies come
and glow!"

He laughed with that, and bowed to her
but the challenge did he see
and so he said: "But one more thing
Would you care to wager me?"

She also laughed with those around
and nodded to his jest
"Yes, I will – three crowns of gold
against your sword and crest!"

"A bet it is! – I'll take that now
and see you late this night
For you and I with servant each
will vouch if you are right!"

The moon so black
the shadows dead
the night like thickened smoke
and add to that a chilling mist
that hung across
the moat

"Oh, what a night to set us out
on such a foolish quest
my bones do chill
this night so damp
No fairies will venture out . . .
even if they do exist!

But a wager made
is a wager done
and so they bundled out
and stumbled on an ancient path
that led thru woods about

"Is this the spot?", in hushed tones said
"Where your fairies come to dance?
it is so bleak and thick with brush
and thorns that cut my pants

But the Queen was firm and serious now
and hushed him with a look
and so they waited
til time stood still
as they leaned
against a nook

And then from naught
slight music played
like prancing in the brain
and flashing lights
danced thru the wood
then gathered in mist soaked rain

And fairies much
like butterflies
came fluttering to the clear
they danced the air
with joyousness
as several drew quite near

And knight moved slight
but ah so quick
to capture one so close
but quicker than the eye could see
all vanished like a ghost

"Pay up, my knight!"
The Queen laughed loud
"For legends have come true!
But, keep your sword
as a lesson learned
forever
that you know"

And so the knight
placed fist on heart
and bowed
with honor said:
"I think, my Queen
a lesson learned
that legends are all
not dead!"

And if a moral
you need be
can come from what you've read
Keep open mind
and open heart
and listen to all
that's said

For fairies
creatures of the night
and others of their kind
although are legends
once were real
but still exist
in mind

Illustration: Original photograph copyright by aralezi on Fotolia by license, and then PhotoShopped by me. The original background image on my website was the inspiration for the poem, and was the image of a gravely injured winged dog with a sword sticking out of a fatal wound, the creature looking skyward as it realizes its fate. The image haunted me for weeks until this poem suddenly appeared. As in all my poems, the inspiration usually hits suddenly, with overwhelming compulsion. (poem 2011)

The Creature

Oh creature as you breathe your last
what foul deed
this day has passed?
Who did this thing to end the life
of such a precious soul?

Who flew the air
who did no harm
you flew to lands no man had gone
to be so slain by sword so quick
the last (of) your magic kind

For men know not
no honor have
to slaughter thus your precious heart

Unto the past you now must pass
a legend now
your life the last

And so you look unto your dreams
and God above
in sadness seems
You leave this Earth
and leave the Land
ne'er to return again

I pray for you
my heart beats low
for this is something that I know
I shall never forget all you were
as you pass
into God's great light

Illustration: The illustration is the Ride of the Valkyries by the English painter John Charles Dollman. (1909). The poem originates with my long time fascination of Viking lore. This is a fantasy poem about the Norse Valkyrie, the beautiful supernatural women who, riding through the sky, would chose from those warriors recently slain in battle, and bring back only the bravest to reside in Valhalla, the home of the gods. The words, rhyme, and spellings were deliberately chosen purely for their effect. I love the sound and tempo of this fantasy/Viking poem. (2011)

Das Valkyrie

She road a horse on thru the sky
and all around the warriors cry
Das Valkyrie! Das Valkyrie!
takes the dead from battle field

Der Valkyrie est beauty fair
Das wind does't blow thru flowing hair
Das Valkyrie! Das Valkyrie!
A shield is by your side

En unt das day in bloody war
das Valkyrie comes thru the moor
Das Valkyrie! Das Valkerie!
Valhalla is your place

Unt none can run
Unt none can hide
from Valkyrie come from der sky
das Valkyrie
das Valkyrie
your sword cannot be stayed

Das ravens fly around your face
your sword does't swing in Odin's grace
das Valkyrie
das Valkyrie
You choose amongst the dead

And warriors soon to Odin's side
das Valkyrie take for that ride
to sit Valhalla to fight once more
at Ragnarok the final score

Oh Valkyrie
Oh Valkyrie
Ein seig you coming on

Illustration: "The Last Day" copyright & created by the amazing Austrian artist, Alexander Kofler. You can see more of his incredible work on his website www.screenpainting.com. The image is a personal favorite of mine, and appears with the specific permission and blessing of the artist. For that, I am deeply indebted. I also use this image for my legal blog. My commentary appears at the end of the poem.

Chivalry is Never Dead!

"Chivalry is never dead!
hand on hilt to varlet said
"Chivalry will never die
but certainly you will!

"How dare you speak to Lady Fair
or even think to touch her hair
This slight will not go unavenged
of that I am
too sure

"So draw your blade and meet your death
you scum of earth
you varlet pest
you have no honor
you have no place
except neath earth
in ground

And with those words
he drew his sword
and smote the varlet
and then his ward
and let their blood
soak all the ground
as warning, yes -
to all around

"For Chivalry
it is my trust
to avenge all maidens
that, I must
and varlets who dwell or
walk these lands
beware
my blade
runs deep

And then the knight
put sword in sheath
and mounted horse
so very neat
and rode away
to castle yon
without a care
or thought

For knights of old
had tempers quick
and always ready
a sword to stick
into most anyone who would offend
their honor, maids, or King

And so this poem ends
as all poems must
but like the knight it gathers dust
and while the pen is mightier
than the sword
that's because
there are no knights
about

Chivalry is Never Dead is a fantasy poem written somewhat tongue-in-cheek, about a knight who with great disdain takes affront to an innocent comment made to a Lady of the Court by a passing commoner — and in the name of "chivalry" strikes both the man and his servant dead, in the middle of the street, then riding off to yonder castle without a passing thought. Of course — there is a warning here: "Don't tick off anyone wearing a sword". There's also a lesson: That while we often remember the glory of this violent Age, we often forget of its sheer brutality, and its callous indifference to life, unless you were a knight, or of noble birth. (2011)

Illustration: Portion of image, "Knight fighting dragon" copyright Dusan Kostic by license from Fotolia. A full image appears at the end of the poem in smaller dimensions. Likewise, my commentary appears at the end of the poem.

Dragon Killer

He stole so quickly thru darkened hall
trodding with care
lest trip or fall

For monster slept both hard and lite
awake by the day
asleep by nite

With rasping breath
he climbed steep path
with ancient sword
does't that . . . he haft

"Oh, magic cloak protect us all!"
lest dragon stir
by yonder wall

Breathing fire
claws of death
bones are scattered
east and west

For those who thought
they'd conquer all
were torn to bits in ashen pall

Then door beyond
of gold and brass
so barred with spells
so none could pass

And yet beyond
rest Magic book
full all of secrets
if he could look

Stealthy, Stealthy . . .
now so slow
only feet and yards
to go

Hear it's breathing
feel the heat
see its talons
scales replete

Almost past the dragon's sleep
slip the lock
so very neat

And the door slid
just a crack
as the dragon's
head reared back

"No!", he cried
and raised his blade
but not enough
he wasn't saved

Fire rang out
and filled the hall
talons ripped
the knight did fall

For the book
was not for him
ancient curse
the room grew dim

And the Dragon
closed its eyes

'Til the next
came there to die

Dragon Killer is a poem about a knight who seeks a book of very valuable spells guarded by a sleeping dragon. He makes the fatal mistake of thinking that getting by a dragon will be easy. Of course, he is sadly mistaken. The dragon has been waiting for him, as it has for so many others before him. All have failed, and this attempt is no different. This accords with my basic philosophy: that if there really were any dragons the way the stories describe them – we'd all be in for a whole lot of trouble. (2011)

Illustration: Cleopatra by the English painter, Thomas Frances Dicksee. (1876). The poem is the story of a deceitful woman who entices the king with her charms, and then kills him. Not sure where the inspiration came from, but it has a King Lear feeling to it. (2014).

The Deadly Plot

She came before the king one day
she said she came from far away
of royal blood that . . . she did say
with eyes that burned like fire

They warned the king she was not true
but skin so smooth, her talk was too
so sensuous he never knew
Her heart was black as stone

For deep within that none could see
there burned a hate, that hate was she
and none could guess Her evil plot
so despicable was Her plan

And so the plot she launched in fact
to kill the king, he'd not come back
and whiled Her way into his bed
and close unto his side

Did none suspect this deed so foul?
in dead of night from earth's dark bowel
and poison . . . did drip in his ear
as he lay there . . . deep in sleep

No sharpened knife could kill as well
as poison from Her blackness fell
upon the light that was his life
as he suddenly came awake

He tried to yell
he tried to rise
he struggled hard to open eyes
and through the haze that stole his life
she laughed as he passed on

And in the morn when she arose
she called up tears as cold as stone
and called the guards, and tearfully cried
"Our king! . . . Our king, has somehow died"

The castle wailed upon his death
it struck their hearts – they'd lost their best
A kingdom now without a king
A loss that all could feel

And so they mourned for seven days
all things turned grey as if a haze
and few could remember what each they did
so great . . . the loss they felt

And all this time she smiled in glee
so masterful Her evil be
and none did guess what she had done
except one faithful knight

And so he stole into Her room
and saw the vial that sealed Her doom
and took it up to mage so great
who knew just what it was

"Take care, good knight, her evil's great
"They think she loved, but it was hate
"And plot she did to kill this king
" And steal his kingdom, fair"

And so they hatched a plot their own
and placed the vial where sure she'd roam
below Her bed where king had died
and watched each day with loyal spies

And then one night she searched the room
and found the vial that sealed Her doom
and picked it up, then hid it quick
but a spy did see it all

And called the guards, and called the mage
and called the evil that was Her name
They took Her there in heavy chains
to dungeon without fail

And in the morn before the court
they called the deed that she had wrought
and cries were heard amongst the crowd
as they demanded that she would die

And bound Her hands
and hung Her high
and let Her swing against the sky
and when her life did leave the earth
their Liege he was avenged

For king was dead forever lost
His nephew took his throne
Such cost!
And never did they err forget
what had happened to their king

And now time ends as years go by
and on this day the kingdom cries
for every year we remember well
when the Evil took our king

The moral?
Do you ask of me?
I'll tell you then so you can see
that never let love blind those, your eyes
to the evil . . . that can line the soul

Of shapely legs, and smooth, smooth skin
of lips that answer your every whim
but love is more
than just the flesh . . .
when a heart is black as stone

Illustration: "Norse man and Woman" by the German painter Johannes Gehrts. (1884). The poem, "The Poison" is allegory. It tells of a queen who's mind is poisoned against her lover by those jealous of his possible influence and interference. In some ways, an allegory of a situation that occurred in my own life many years ago. The "poison" are the lies spread by others, to their disgrace, and purely for their own advantage and purpose. (2014)

The Poison

The poison swirled inside her head
she hardly knew she'd soon be dead
as thoughts which entered and swirled around
soon killed the love that she had found

It was their duty, or so they said
these things they whispered inside her head
but lies were told again, again
they feared this love she'd found

And poison works as poison grows
the beating heart it slowly slows
until there's not a thing to see
the poison works so silently

And so her love
the deepening bliss
she sent away without a kiss
and never did she ever say
why he was sent so far away

And all her court did gather round
and swore that they were honor bound
to tell the truth and keep her safe
but lied instead to their disgrace

And assured her this and every day
t'was better off with him away
While each one watched their poison grow
as her joy began to fade

And now she walks the path alone
no one to kiss
no one to hold
and dreams the dream
that never was
as mist it gathers round

Illustration: Sleepwalker by the Czech painter, Maximilian Pirner. (1853) My commentary appears at the end of the poem.

The Dream

She was sleeping
deeply
dreaming dreams of things
so long ago
things that were
and never were
and those that could have been
for she was old now
and while there were those who loved her
many had passed
and others were too far away
and so
she was alone

A mirror appeared
and she looked in it
what she saw was not unpleasing
yes, older
but kind
and good
and despite all these years
there was an inner and outer beauty
that shone thru
and burned bright
but also there was a sadness
for something was missing

Suddenly the mist of time appeared
swirling around her
until so thick that nothing could be seen
or heard
or even imagined

And then the mist suddenly cleared
and she found herself in a hallway
that went on forever

And she did not know what to do
and for the first time in her life
she was afraid
for she was alone
in a place so strange
that it seemed
without end

And then she felt a hand in hers
and a soothing voice spoke to her
and she felt immediately calm
and warm
and good
and safe
and knew for the first time
that she was not alone
and never would be
but still − she could not see him
for he was hidden

And she called to him saying
"Who are you , and how did you get here? "
And the voice laughed softly
with a gentleness that warmed her soul
and said: "Do not fear, my love,
"For I am always with thee
"None can do you harm
"For I watch over you "

And with that she awoke
alone in her bed
Wishing . . .
she were back
in the dream

The Dream is both a fantasy poem and a love poem. It tells the story of a woman grown older, still beautiful, who is haunted in a dream by a past love who continues to watch over her — whom she realizes she dearly misses, only upon coming awake. It is an allegory of a part of my life, perhaps a bit too personal to share beyond that. One of the most popular fantasy poems on my website. (2011)

Illustration: The image is "Dragon Hunt", copyright vukkostic by license from Fotolia. "The Captive Wizard" is a fantasy poem about a powerful wizard who allows himself to be captured in order to seek retribution on behalf of himself and all other travelers in a kingdom unjustly ruled by an evil queen. Like many of my other poems, it is an allegory. It was inspired by my frustration with a court case, and the judge I was trying the case before. I thought her unfair and unfeeling, and every time I went into court it felt like a never-ending uphill battle. Of course, there was no way to retaliate, and so I took out my frustration by writing the poem. In the end, I won the case in a trial, and also won the judge over to my side. (2011)

The Captive Wizard

The man was taken off his horse
as he traveled thru the land
he said he had done nothing wrong
he did not understand

"You failed to pay
"You failed to bow
"and so you broke our law
"I seize your horse and all you own
"and still, there's so much more!"

"But I protest. This is not fair
"I intended no such slight
"I am a wizard from a far off land
"I'll be gone before dawn's light!"

The warrior smashed him deftly hard
he staggered to the ground
the blood ran from the wound it left
his hands were stoutly bound

Then dragged behind the warriors horse
back to the castle tall
he ran along as best he could
lest dragged if he should fall

"What have we here?" the guard called out
"A prisoner for our queen?
"We'll hang him high inside the court
"we'll stretch that neck quite lean!"

They took him then
and threw him down unto a dungeon deep
but smile he did
when no one watched
and then did fall asleep

And woken in the morning light
and taken 'fore the queen
her hair was black with narrow eyes
her countenance was quite mean

"How dare you, sir, come in my land
"and not my homage do?
"you shall be hanged upon the morn
"your head be cut askew"

He looked at her, and then around
his eyes began to glow
blue fire then surrounded him
that all who looked should know

"It's not my time, but, it is yours!
"You've upset the powers that be!
"You've captured here a wizard great . . .
"You should have set me free!"

The sky drew dark
thick clouds appeared
and thunder sounded round
and lightening bolts did fill the sky
and deftly struck the ground

"I frighten not!" yelled the queen
enraged at what she saw
"No, wizard will overpower me
"I'd rather wager war!"

And then a dragon appeared from air
and grabbed her by the head
and shook it twice
then ripped it off
yes . . . she was surely dead

The warriors who had mistreated him
were burned to ash and dust
the chains that had once bound him there
fell off, all turned to rust

Those who survived bowed to the mage
and begged him "Please, forgive!"
They held hands out, and swore an oath
if He would let them live

He raised his hands unto the sky
and dragon swooped to ground
it dropped the head of evil queen
the rest, was never found

"I let you live upon this day
"but your castle is destroyed
"your laws were bad
"your queen was worse
"you had me quite annoyed!

"So, I did come
"to teach you all
"a lesson to be learned
"that those who harm a traveler
"will have their castles burned!"

And then the mage
turned into light
it almost made them blind
but on a rock near rubbled wall
did this inscription find:

"Let no man harm a traveler
or dragons will appear
For wizards roam these lands you have
of Them
you best have fear"

Illustration: Planet Earth Sunrise, copyright sdecoret by license from Shutterstock. My commentary appears after the conclusion of the poem.

Star Bender

Star Bender
keeper of dreams
Timeless Being who floats between worlds unseen
what see You now
what worlds do You travel
what galaxies do You seek?

For when You dream
worlds change
a universe implodes
and all things are created
from nothing

Star Bender
how many others
like You
are there?

Oh, Star Bender
can you see what you have created
or does it really matter
for what in a millisecond of Your time
do a thousand years
pass by

Star Bender
what powers You grant
to this poor mortal
on this poor earthen planet?

(and the Star Bender replied:)

"Oh, Mortal
You ask what powers I bestow?

"To you
I bestow life
and all it has to offer
I bestow ability

"I bestow thought
I bestow love
I bestow the ability to create more
of who you are

"What you do with these gifts
that is for you to decide
for what I have done
is enough
And now
you must make your own journey
to the stars"

And with that
the Star Bender
in a millisecond of thought . . .
moved on
to another dream
timeless
forever

"Star Bender" is both a fantasy poem, science fiction poem, and spiritual poem. It is a throwback to some of my earlier poetry, similar to what I was writing before law school. The poem is a conversation that takes place in a millisecond of thought, within a dream, between an earth mortal, and a Supreme Being traveling between the stars. It asks and answers the eternal question of who we are, and what is our future – with the answer that whatever our future is – that is entirely up to us. (2011)

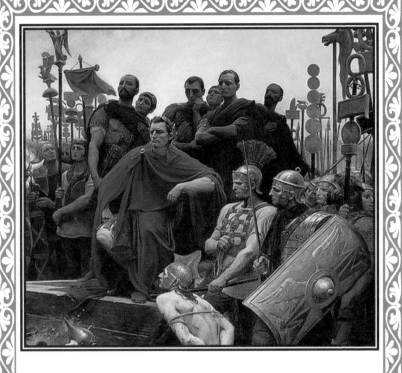

Illustration: The illustration shows a portion of the painting "Vercingetorix Surrenders to Caesar", by the French painter, Lionel Royer. (1899) The poem, "The Conquest", is an allegory of my frustration with our political system, and how the failure of our elected officials to work together for the common good vs. their own personal and party aspirations will lead to disaster. Rome conquered a world because those they fought could not band together against the invading Romans, such was their hated for one another. In many ways, an analogy. (2011).

The Conquest

The warriors were divided on
how to attack
some said to go forward
some said to go back
others insisted to outflank was best
others were certain
"Attack from the West"

Their leaders divided
they soon came to blows
some would not speak
others did go . . .
Back to their towns
Back to their lands
carrying their pennants
rather than stand

And all of this time
the enemy – grew
Lines neat and ordered
and each of them
knew

How to attack
how to destroy
not one of them argued
not one of them toyed

For each in that legion
were disciplined men
they had but one purpose
to win in the end

They obeyed each their Consul
who dictated all
and each worked together
lest all of them fall

And on that bright morning
they pushed thru the land
and fought not an army
though brave
to the man

For only together
could any withstand
their hundreds of lines
their thousands of man

All dressed in their armor
their greaves and their helm
With shields locked together
their swords overwhelm

They shouted as one
they advanced like a storm
and those who opposed them
t'was like
shearing corn

And when it was over
the slaughter was quick
the bodies lay lifeless
too many to pick

Their land was not theirs
they'd lost what they had
through bickering
indecision
it truly
was sad

And brought forth in chains
all but the dead
to the Consul who'd won
to the survivors
he said:

"You either swear homage
"to Me on this day
"or I'll burn each your towns
"and sweep you
"away

"You all were not worthy
"You had not a plan
"We battled you down
"Each knight and
"Each man

"For only together
can an army survive
you work all as one
or don't
stay alive

"And now those
your kingdoms
Are Ours – for you've lost
you failed to unite
you've paid
quite a cost

"And Rome again conquers
lands ruled by just tribes
our legions are great
our Empire thrives

"A lesson to all
who want to be free
work together as one
or defeat . . .
shall it be"

Illustration: The "Viking Ships" by the American painter Edward Moran. (1860). I was looking at images of Viking ships when a thunder storm rolled in, and this poem was the result. I consider the poem almost a chant, which I find calming to repeat when a violent storm approaches. (2011)

The Storm Gods

The Storm Gods They cometh
They bringeth the rain
Thor's hammer doest pound
again and again

The thunderclaps strong
the lightening bolts strike
the animals shudder
all huddled with fright

Oh, Odin! - Oh, Odin!
Protect us from harm!
call on the Heros
save our ships and our farms

For the Jotnar are angry
the Giants are quick
they throw their bolts at us
the rain comes too slick

And as we ride out the rough of the storm
we drink quaffs of Ale until it's all gone

And then in the distance
the thunder recedes
the clouds break for moonlight
which comes thru with ease
the stars shine their pathways
the waves cease to roll
the ships lie at anchor
their bells do not toll

And fall we asleep, as fires all die down
while sentries do watch
now safe
all around

Illustration: Excerpt from "The Battle of Grunwald" by Jan Matzjeko. (1874). The poem tells about the Battle of Stamford Bridge in 1066, where a single Viking warrior held back the army of King Godwinson of England from the retreating Vikings for almost an hour. He was finally cut down, and Godwinson's army destroyed the fleeing invading army. (2011)

The Warrior of Stamford Bridge

He fought thru death with axe, no shield
though overwhelmed he would not yield
and on that bridge he stood as stone
for none would he let pass

They sent their best in two's and three's
he fought them there
struck thru their greaves
and armor did not stop his swing
or the power of his resolve

For he was one against them all
he would not stop, he would not fall
or let the them pass
or let them go
for he was there to stay

And then a lull did slowly come
where men had fought
and some had run
and high above on wayward hill
the Saxon King did watch

King Godwinson sat on steed in awe
his army stopped, of that – he saw
by a single Viking, a warrior true
This man, did not deserve to die

"Take this message to that man:
Put down your arms and take my hand
and join my army at my side
In this way I would spare and honor you"

The courier took the message fast
unto the bridge, thru uncut grass
and there he raced neath flag of white
and from his horse he did alight

"Oh, warrior who is brave and true
My king gives Honor direct to you
For brave you are beyond all men
your death would not be fair

"Please take your leave and freedom, too
or join us here as a warrior true
For men like you are few and far
Of this you can be sure"

The warrior thought then shook his head
and looked around at all the dead
then looked upon the hill and King
and said these fateful words:

"Your king is great. He honors me
And vast your army that, do I see
but I cannot forsake my oath
no matter what the cost"

The courier nodded and raised his hand
put fist to chest to salute the man
and then rode back to tell his king
of what he had been told

"Take archers hence, three score or more
and cut him down to end this war
for though he die I'll cross that bridge
My reign it shall endure"

And so the sky turned black with spear
the arrows coming ever near
until like rain they pierced and slew
and down He went
his life was through

And there was silence
no words were spoke
These men he fought this place remote

And carried him
to top of hill
as an honor for all to see

And in a voice heard all around
the Saxon king
his heart did pound
did honor this brave, fallen man
for his army, and all to see

And when t'was over
the king moved on
the other army fled, not gone
but they were caught and overwhelmed
then slaughtered to the man

Now centuries passed
this place known not
these kings long dead
their names forgot
but on that hill on stones pilled high
this story lives
it cannot die

For a warrior so brave
His honor fast
Who'd rather fight unto his last
than surrender there though overwhelmed
for all around
did see

I remember you well
Oh, Valiant Man
Who stood alone
with axe in hand
And to all those men
who wavered not
At Stamford Bridge
that day

Illustration: Photoshop by me from painting by
academic French painter, William Adolphe
Bourguereau, date unknown. My commentary
follows the conclusion of the poem.

So Long Ago

So long ago
so long ago
across the ice
and blowing snow
as if a dream
a dream I know
so long ago
so long ago

I met a girl of flaxen hair
she held my hand
to everywhere
she stole my heart
she stole my soul
so long ago
so long ago

I saw her photo in the news
she took a flight
and then a cruise
but it went down
in water deep
so far away its secrets keep
so long ago
so long ago

They sent their ships
they sent their planes
they looked that night
and then for days
but nothing did they ever see
but sky and waves
upon the sea
so long ago
so long ago

They called the search
and shook their heads
so many lost
presumed them dead
and none were found
not one
not ten
so long ago
so long ago

We laid some flowers on the sea
and thought of her
and where she'd be
and hoped it was not
painfully slow
the flowers drifted
so long ago
Ah, yes . . . it was
so long ago

I keep her photo
close to me
and feel the pain
that all can see
and yes, I see love in her eyes
she keeps my heart
until I die
so long ago
so long ago

And now I'm old
I'll soon pass on
to where . . . know not
but I'll be gone
and all this time she's in my dreams
she whispers soft
and fills my needs
so long ago
so long ago

I feel so strange
I feel so down
the room spins suddenly
all around
and on the floor
I rest my head
and then I know
that I am
dead
so long ago
so long ago

And then she comes
thru air and time
I take her hand
pressed into mine
and then we leave
into the light
and pass thru time
with all things right
so long ago
so long ago

Commentary: This haunting fantasy love poem
spans a lifetime, and gives you the feeling of going in
and out of a dream. It tells the tale of two lovers,
separated by time and a terrible disaster at sea,
where one of them is lost, forever. In many ways,
like the Titanic. The other can never forget his lost
love, and she stays with him in mind, until he too,
finally passes. The end of the poem is deeply
spiritual, and completes the story of these two lovers
— joining them in a place beyond time . . . in God's
great grace, forever. (2012)

Illustration: Excerpt from painting, "Heart of Snow" by the pre-Raphaelite English painter Edward Robert Hughes. (1907). The poem is an allegory of someone I cared for dearly who made a choice. You'll have to speculate on anything beyond that as it is deeply personal, as is this poem. (2013)

Alone

She sits on a mountain surrounded by snow
it is a place only she can go
and there up high in frozen bliss
she wonders now
if she will miss

The life she left if life could be
in warmth of sand
by breeze of sea
and holding the hand of who she loved
now lost
now lost
in time

Now snowflakes swirl and gather round
the path that led cannot be found
and deeper, deeper
snow grows deep
so every day
her secrets keep

And looks around this place so bare
as white does streak once golden hair
and lines invade a perfect face
all tempered in the snow's embrace

For she lives alone
upon the steep
has given all
but did not keep
what she loved best
and let him go
forever left in deepening snow
forever left
alone

Illustration: Trees near valley. Copyright Pellinni by license from Fotolia. The poem "Rainbow Bridge", is based on a story by William S. Britton. The story has many versions by many authors. While the idea of the "rainbow bridge" originates from Norse mythology and was the magical bridge between the realm of the Gods and that of man – the current version tells of a wondrous place where beloved pets go after their deaths only to be reunited with their loving master or mistress when all have passed. (2012)

Rainbow Bridge – a poem

They say a place called Rainbow Bridge
is somewhere in the sky
it is a place where loving pets
go after they do die

Its meadows and its green fields
are surrounded by rolling hills
the sky is clear
the moon is bright
pets heal without their ills

And each day that they stay there
they play and romp with fun
and in the night thru God's Great Grace
sleep sound 'til morning comes

And there they stay while time stands still
until the day you die
and then a light does suddenly shine
and your pet begins to cry

For it sees you in the clearing
so far but yet so near
and runs to you with wagging tail
without a care or fear

And then it jumps into your arms
warm kisses on your face
it quivers with excitement now
to feel your fond embrace

For love will always triumph
the bond will never break
and side-by-side
cross Rainbow Bridge
which leads
to Heaven's Gate

Illustration: Road across Alien Landscape. Copyright by Angela Harburn, licensed through Fotolia. The poem, like the movie "2001 – A Space Odyssey" tells of a strange monolith hidden deep on the moon. But, in this case, it is a gift from another civilization that guards Earth from alien invaders. (2010)

The Monolith

The monolith stands on the moon
so bleak and bare with ancient rune
carved laser like in perfect row
what story can it possibly stow?

Of ancient ones
of Those from space
who fathered this – the human race?

And if they've gone
gone to where
are any left
do any care?

For Monolith stands guard above
perhaps a token of their love
and unseen beam surrounds us all
its powers yet unknown

No invading force has come this way
the Monolith has barred their stay
their starships lost
their travels blocked
the Monolith stands tall

Yet silent moon
no rush or breeze
but empty valleys and mountains seize
the senses all on this bleak place
the emptiness of space

And yet it watches and sees all
yes, programed for one urgent call
decisions light years far away
to a race we'll never know

But yes, they watch
and yes, they care
and yes, they travel
here and where
but never will we ever be
what may have created
you
and me

And the Monolith
it stands

Illustration: Noc (ie: Night) by the English painter, Edward Robert Hughes. The poem, an interpretation of the serenity, fantasy and escape of the dream. (2011)

A Winter Dream
We close our eyes
we fall asleep
and all through winter
fond dreams we keep

Of stars
and dragons
of moon
and sky

Until we wake
until we die

Of all those things
we loved most dear
until tomorrow
exist
so clear

- The end -

About the Poet

Jon Gutmacher lives in Florida, and is a retired criminal trial attorney who is also well known in Florida as a expert in the field of firearm, weapon, and self defense laws, and has published a popular book on the subject. He started writing poetry back in junior high school when inspired to do so in an English literature class, and continued to dabble with it until entering law school. For a brief period he wrote a weekly poetry column for The Ojus Sun, a local arts newspaper in the Miami area back in the early 1970's.

The first book he ever read as a child was "The Boys King Arthur" which featured the incredible illustrations of N.C. Wyeth, and which ignited a love of both fantasy, history, and science fiction that lasts thru today. Since that early introduction he continued to read all he could in this genre of fiction until entering law school.

Of course, law school and law left very little time for anything else, and until a very painful shoulder surgery in 2010, Mr. Gutmacher discontinued his involvement with poetry, and the casual reading of fantasy and other novels. Law became the focus of his life. However, the long recovery period that followed the surgery gave him a different outlook on life, where other things became more important than the practice of law. The result was that he started writing poetry again, and began a website for his poems in late 2010, which was soon ranked by Google as one of the top five "fantasy poetry" websites in the nation, and since 2011 has been consistently ranked either #1 or #2 in that genre. This is his first poetry book.